Welcome to solopreneurship,

the epic rollercoaster ride that involves doing *all the things*, often all by ourselves, in pursuit of passion, impact, and freedom. Where the to-do lists are endless, the nights can be long, and we're forever explaining what the heck we do for a living.

After years and years in business there's an unexpected thing I've learned: mindset matters just as much, if not more, than strategy. All the webinars, social media posts, and email funnels won't help if you're continuously doubting yourself or worrying that it won't work.

Because I've found so much help in a daily journaling practice myself, I wanted to take my giant collection of prompts and make them available to you, my ambitious friend.

Studies have shown that journaling helps bring you into a state of mindfulness which can reduce anxiety and negative thoughts, and can actually reduce how often those issues pop into your mind throughout the day. Writing down your goals signals your brain that those things are important and increases your likelihood of achieving them. Plus starting one healthy habit tends to spread healthy habits into other areas of your life!

Sometimes we are so in our businesses that we don't make time to step back and analyze our thoughts, our actions, and look at the big picture, so my recommendation for using this journal is to carve out 20 minutes every day (EVERY day - you can do it!) and challenge yourself to spend 100 days knocking out the 100 prompts.

If a prompt doesn't apply to you, write the opposite (What's holding you back from hitting your deadlines? vs Why are you a rockstar at hitting your deadlines?). Or go for my favorite prompt which you'll find repeated throughout this journal: *I'm grateful for, I desire, I'm already rocking at*.

My hope is that you'll find some clarity and relief among these pages which will contribute to you not only growing your business but feeling like a badass boss as you do it!

Cheers to your success!

XO Sarah

P.S. I'd LOVE to see how you're using the journal and what you're learning so feel free to share a photo and tag me at @xosarahmorgan.

Who are you dedicated to helping + why is that important to you?

empty nesters, growing old in place + families living organized + functionally beautiful lives.

affordable, functional beauty

→ because I personally find it overwhelming + depressing to live w/o it.

How are you different from other people in your niche / industry?

I'm not sure that I am.

List all the things you rocked in the past year and the things you could have done better . . .

What personal beliefs / traits will help to make you + your business a success?

What is something you are totally overthinking + how can you get past it?

What will make your clients / customers obsessed with what they're working toward?

What could your life + business look like at the next level? *(Be super detailed with this one!)*

When you notice a negative feeling, what are you focusing on that might not be true?

List 20 ways you help your clients or customers get what they want . . .

I am grateful for . . . _____

_____
_____
_____
_____
_____
_____
_____
_____

I desire . . . _____

_____
_____
_____
_____
_____
_____
_____
_____

I am already rocking at . . . _____

_____
_____
_____
_____
_____
_____
_____

> **Boss up and change your life. You can have it all, no sacrifice.**
>
> **LIZZO**

I'm expert enough and in the right space to accomplish my goals because . . .

_____
_____
_____
_____
_____
_____
_____
_____
_____
_____
_____
_____
_____
_____
_____
_____
_____
_____
_____
_____
_____
_____
_____
_____
_____
_____
_____

What do you know you should be doing but are putting off? What would happen if you did it?

I'm deciding that _____ is totally possible for me because . . .

What would make you so obsessed with your biz that you can't wait to start every day?

What is holding you back from consistently hitting your deadlines?

List 20 ways you can improve your content, sales, email marketing, social media . . .

What actions can you take to show up more + play bigger?

At the end of your career what words + actions do you want to be known for?

How are you + your business changing lives?

I am grateful for . . . _____

_____
_____
_____
_____
_____
_____
_____
_____

I desire . . . _____

_____
_____
_____
_____
_____
_____
_____
_____

I am already rocking at . . . _____

_____
_____
_____
_____
_____
_____
_____

"

Don't be intimidated by what you don't know. That can be your greatest strength + ensure that you do things differently from everyone else.

SARA BLAKELY

What are your limiting beliefs around showing up more + being seen?

Describe a client / customer success and how they've been impacted by what you do . . .

What is something you're worried about sharing with your audience?

List your goals for the next 3 months, 1 year, and 3 years . . .

Affirmation time! List 20 positive "I am" statements . . .

What does your life look like running the business of your dreams?

Who have you been today that you're proud of?

What's holding you back from being productive?

What do you need to do to make your business exactly the way you want it?

I am grateful for . . . _____

_____
_____
_____
_____
_____
_____
_____

I desire . . . _____

_____
_____
_____
_____
_____
_____
_____

I am already rocking at . . . _____

_____
_____
_____
_____
_____
_____
_____

> "
> **The willingness to show up changes us. It makes us a little braver each time.**
>
> **— BRENÉ BROWN**

What's one thing you need to learn or work on to improve your business?

What thoughts + feelings will you focus on to get what you want today?

What are you afraid would happen if your next project / launch was a massive success?

What would you do if you already had $5 million sitting in the bank . . .

List at least 20 ways to nail your next goal . . .

What would you do if there were no rules and you knew you could not fail . . .

I forgive myself for . . .

What habits + experiences does the next-level version of you prioritize?

What stressful thoughts consistently show up in your life + what do they make you do or not do?

I am grateful for . . . _____

_____
_____
_____
_____
_____
_____
_____
_____

I desire . . . _____

_____
_____
_____
_____
_____
_____
_____
_____

I am already rocking at . . . _____

_____
_____
_____
_____
_____
_____
_____

> *If people are doubting how far you can go, go so far that you can't hear them anymore.*
>
> — **MICHELLE RUIZ**

What would you do if your next launch was a guaranteed success . . .

What is your lower self worried about? What would your higher self say + do about that?

What limiting beliefs about yourself + your business is it time to leave behind?

List all your accomplishments . . . *(Yes, even that 5th grade spelling bee you little rockstar)*

At the next level: How would you invest, show up on social media, and take action?

What are the next 3 steps you can take toward your goal and how can you make it super easy?

What part of you doesn't want your goal + what negative things do you think would happen if you accomplished it?

How will your customers or clients be more successful if YOU are more successful?

What parts of running your business do you despise and how can you ditch them?

I am grateful for . . . _____

_____
_____
_____
_____
_____
_____
_____
_____

I desire . . . _____

_____
_____
_____
_____
_____
_____
_____
_____

I am already rocking at . . . _____

_____
_____
_____
_____
_____
_____
_____
_____

"

We need to get women to the point where they aren't apologizing. It is time to take ownership in our success.

TORY BURCH

Who is the last person that benefited from what you teach / sell / share and how?

Describe your perfect work day in detail . . .

How are you worthy of success *(even if you screwed up in the past)?*

Who do you look up to and what habits + traits can you borrow for your own success?

What about your niche / industry drives you freaking crazy?? *(It probably drives your audience crazy as well - talk about it!)*

Who benefits from you showing up + selling?

What would happen if you sold to your audience every day for a month?

Write 20 "I believe" statements and list why . . .
(Ex: I believe journaling is totally life changing!)

What could you have done better in the past week? *(No pity party allowed - it's just info)*

I am grateful for . . . _____

_____
_____
_____
_____
_____
_____
_____
_____

I desire . . . _____

_____
_____
_____
_____
_____
_____
_____
_____

I am already rocking at . . . _____

_____
_____
_____
_____
_____
_____
_____
_____

> "Whatever it is that you think you want to do, and whatever it is that you think stands between you + that, stop making excuses. You can do anything.

— KATIA BEAUCHAMP

You just earned $10k / $50k / $100k in ONE month - how does it feel??

List 20 reasons you will become a success . . .

If you could create, do, launch anything in the next month with zero limits, what would it be?

What seems really challenging right now but you know you could probably make it happen?

List at least 20 "I am willing to" statements . . .
(Ex: I am willing to journal every damn day!)

What does your audience need to hear from you today?

What parts of running your business do you freaking LOVE??

Who are you if you're NOT struggling and your to-do list is easy?

Who supports you in growing your business + how? Whose lack of support isn't helping?

I am grateful for . . . _____

_____
_____
_____
_____
_____
_____
_____
_____

I desire . . . _____

_____
_____
_____
_____
_____
_____
_____
_____

I am already rocking at . . . _____

_____
_____
_____
_____
_____
_____
_____
_____

> *We need to accept that we won't always make the right decisions... Understand that failure is not the opposite of success, it's part of success.*

ARIANNA HUFFINGTON

If you could do anything, what would your daily routine look like?

What messy pieces of your life + experience make you better at your job?

List at least 20 reasons you're a total rockstar at what you do . . .

Who are your dream collaborators, interviews, conferences, events, mentors, experiences?

What do you need to START or STOP doing to create more time in your week?

How do you want clients / customers to feel when working with you or using your products?

At the end of this year what do you want to be most proud of?

What did you do / not do this week that made you feel like a BOSS or a failure?

Who were you before you felt judgement? What did you love and how did you act?

I am grateful for . . . _____

_____
_____
_____
_____
_____
_____
_____
_____

I desire . . . _____

_____
_____
_____
_____
_____
_____
_____
_____

I am already rocking at . . . _____

_____
_____
_____
_____
_____
_____
_____
_____

> **What are you willing to give up to have the life you keep pretending to want?**
>
> — ELIZABETH GILBERT

Think of something that's coming up for your biz and write out the best possible outcome . . .

Whether you're a day in or 10 years, what have you learned since you started your business?

What have you been ignoring in terms of business, self care, and relationships?

How does your audience benefit from you selling to them?

What are you holding back from doing even though you really want to or know it will help?

Pick an entrepreneur and list all the things you admire about them + their business.

What does your business need from you this week to keep running on schedule?

Which of your current limitations can you work through or ditch completely + how?

What does future you need you to start focusing on TODAY?

I am grateful for . . . _____
_____
_____
_____
_____
_____
_____
_____

I desire . . . _____
_____
_____
_____
_____
_____
_____
_____

I am already rocking at . . . _____
_____
_____
_____
_____
_____
_____

> **Every woman's success should be an inspiration to another. We're strongest when we cheer each other on.**
>
> **— SERENA WILLIAMS**

What is your current goal + why have you not accomplished it already?

Who is the next level version of you? What will you have, be, and do?

Consider the last few things that didn't work - what were the lessons you needed to learn?

What business "shoulds" is it time to give up?

What would your 10-year-old self say about your current life + biz?

What patterns or repeat habits can you find with your last 3 projects / goals?

Why are YOU the best person to guide your clients / customers?

What stops you from feeling more confident and powerful?

If you could do anything, what would your weekly routine look like?

I am grateful for . . . _____

_____
_____
_____
_____
_____
_____
_____
_____

I desire . . . _____

_____
_____
_____
_____
_____
_____
_____
_____

I am already rocking at . . . _____

_____
_____
_____
_____
_____
_____
_____

> **You can't make decisions based on fear and the possibility of what might happen.**
>
> — MICHELLE OBAMA

Made in the USA
Coppell, TX
09 October 2020